MUTTS

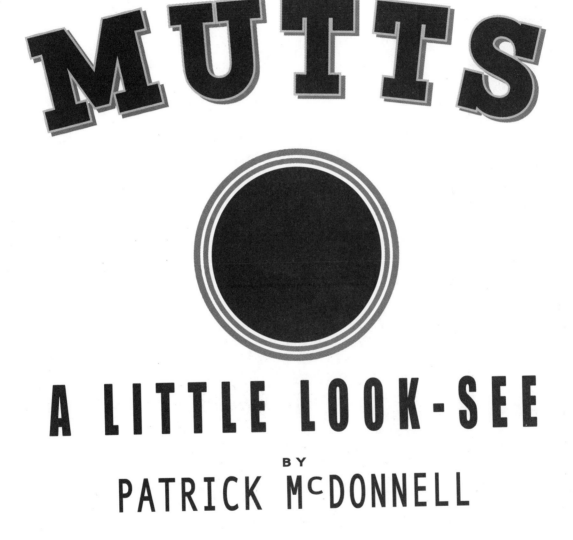

A LITTLE LOOK-SEE

BY
PATRICK M^cDONNELL

**Andrews McMeel
Publishing**

Kansas City

Other Books by Patrick McDonnell

Mutts
Cats and Dogs: Mutts II
More Shtuff: Mutts III
Yesh!: Mutts IV
Our Mutts: Five

Mutts Sundays
The Mutts Little Big Book

Mutts is distributed internationally by King Features Syndicate, Inc. For information write King Features Syndicate, Inc., 235 East 45th Street, New York, New York 10017.

01 02 03 04 05 BAH 10 9 8 7 6 5 4 3 2 1

ISBN: 0-7407-1394-9

Library of Congress Catalog Card Number: 00-108458

A Little Look-See is printed on recycled paper.

ATTENTION: SCHOOLS AND BUSINESSES

Andrews McMeel books are available at quantity discounts with bulk purchase for educational, business, or sales promotional use. For information, please write to: Special Sales Department, Andrews McMeel Publishing, 4520 Main Street, Kansas City, Missouri 64111.

EARL   MOOCH

OZZIE   FRANK   MILLIE   BUTCHIE   DOOZY

GUARDDOG   SID   SHTINKY   NOODLES   WOOFIE

SOURPUSS   CHIPPY   CRABBY   LOLLIPOP   MUSSELS

PHILIPPE   PHOEBE   SHNELLY   BUSHY   SQUIRRELS

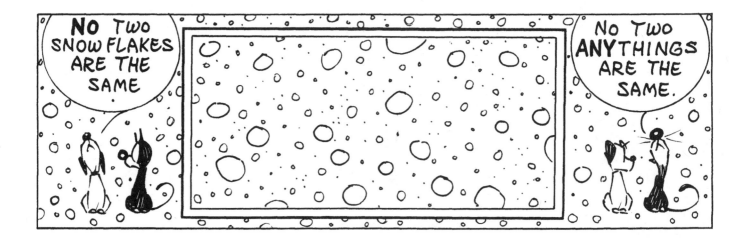

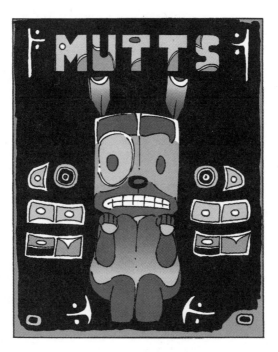

mutts

12

18

23

25

35

40

SHELTER STORIES: PERSONALS

Starting Over - SWF, highly intelligent, attractive, well-traveled, speaks French. Looking for that certain someone who still believes in love. Is it you?

SHELTER STORIES: PERSONALS

Sweet Brown Eyes - I am nine years young - petite, fetching, radiant, yet down to earth. Looking for a committed relationship. No psychos or phonies, please.

SHELTER STORIES: PERSONALS

Me: Warmhearted, spirited, fun, affectionate, waiting.
You: Kind, genuine, tender, compassionate, come and get me.

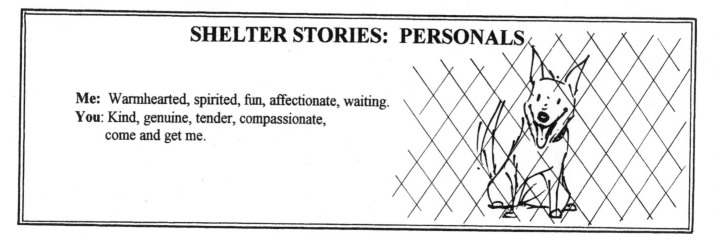

SHELTER STORIES: PERSONALS

Lonely? Me too - Recent orphan wants to love again. Seeks soul mate for a new beginning. You will not believe your luck.

SHELTER STORIES: PERSONALS

Young and handsome - Fun-loving, easygoing, possesses adventuresome spirit. Believes a positive attitude is the key to life. Loves the great outdoors and the Sunday funnies. Let's grow old together.

SHELTER STORIES: PERSONALS

Exotic Long-Hair Beauty - I'd like to inspire you to slow down the hectic pace so we can discover each other. I like long naps, cozy nights, sunny spots, sushi.

MUTTS
COMICUS STRIPUS

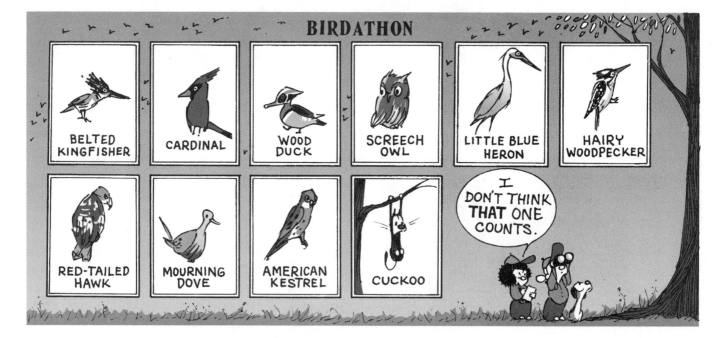

49

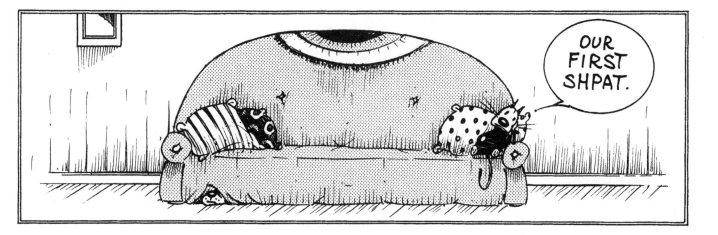

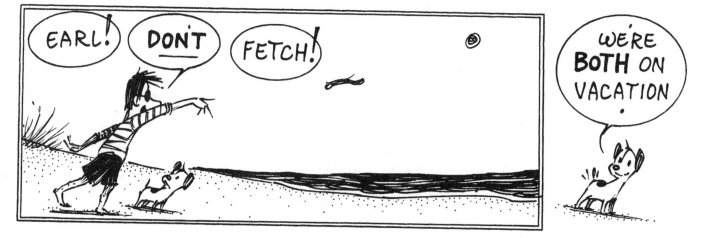

70

74

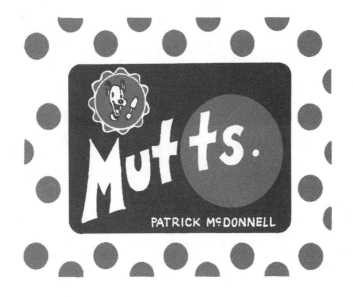

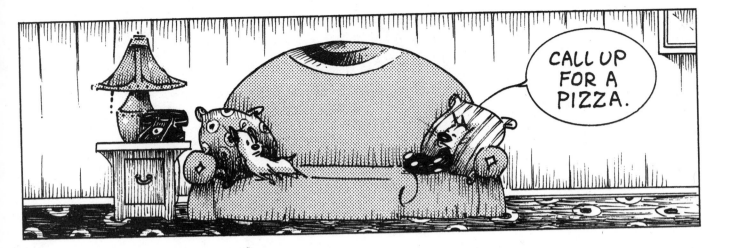

· MUTTS ·

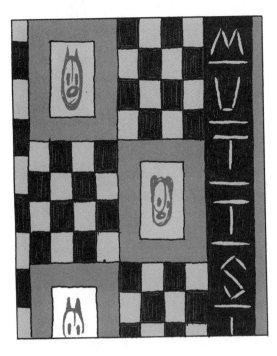

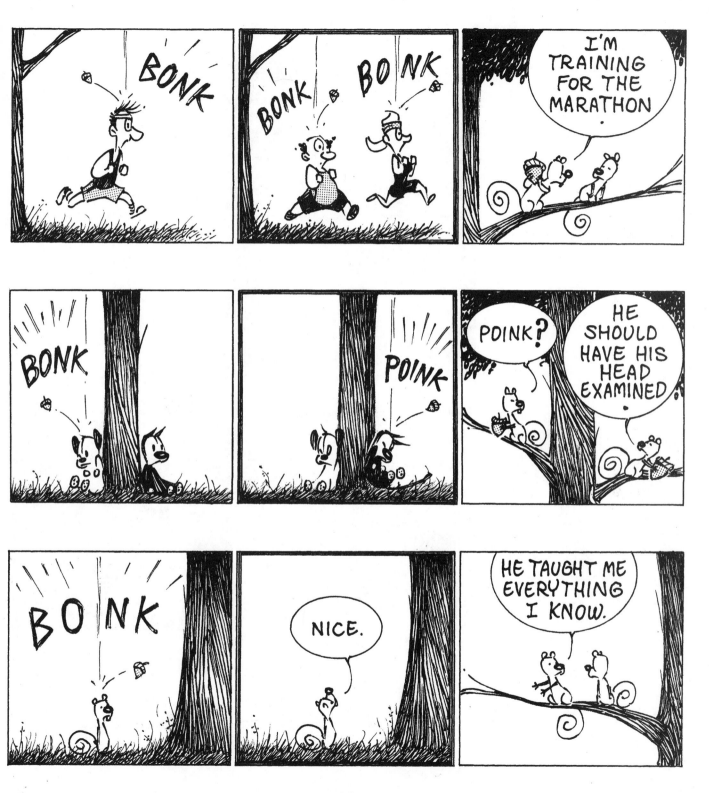

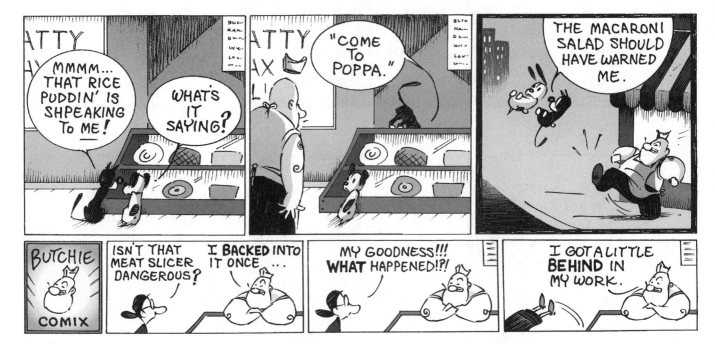

105

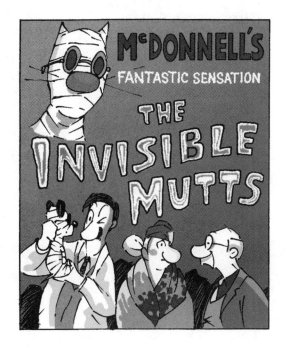

123